Number Wonder

Teaching Basic Math Concepts to Preschoolers

by Jane Jarrell and Deborah Saathoff

Published by Broadman & Holman Publishers, Nashville, Tennessee

ISBN 0-8054-0360-4

Note to Parents and Teachers

There's wonder in numbers and it is our goal to help you introduce your children to the wonder-full numbers all around them every day. We have chosen activities and lessons that are not only fun but help children recognize numerals, number groups, build counting skills, and one-to-one correspondence.

Any time your young child considers more or less, before and after, sorts items, makes sets, finds pairs, puts something in order, identifies parts of a whole, recognizes a pattern, counts, or recognizes numbers he is working on skills that help to lay a strong foundation of skills necessary for learning math concepts.

Young children constantly encounter these activities as a natural part of each day. They recognize a pattern of polka dots on a favorite shirt and numbers on a car's license plate. They encounter toys that are both light and heavy, they eat fruit cut in half, sort blocks, and measure ingredients. Just counting the road signs on the way to the grocery store or making domino cookies can help make the associations fun and memorable.

We have tried to suggest simple and enjoyable activities to help reinforce these concepts naturally throughout the child's daily routine. These activities are grouped in the following divisions:

 Games: Playing games with your children, such as dominoes, card games, or board games can help reinforce number skills and create memories.

 Arts and Crafts: Math and art make a great combination. Learning numbers by designing sculptures and making beads out of edible play dough help create a perfect medium for math appreciation.

 Food: Simple recipes you can prepare with your child while at the same time emphasizing number skills are included in this section. Each recipe gives you a list of needed utensils, ingredients, and directions.

 Home and Community: Numbers are everywhere and in almost every daily activity. Some simple ways to highlight those opportunities found at home in chores and toys, in the grocery store, running errands, and walking in your neighborhood are given here.

 Books and Songs: Books and music enrich every child's day. Book titles that relate to numbers and counting are listed. Counting and number songs and rhymes make singing about math fun anytime. Suggestions on locating the books and songs are given with each section.

 Devotions: A short devotion on a biblical topic for your child is also included with a Scripture reference for each devotion.

An activity page to reinforce the highlighted numbers are given for the numbers one through twelve. The topics for each number correspond to the devotion included for that number.

These ideas are presented to help you create fun-filled moments for you and your child that will reinforce pre-math skills. Don't feel limited to the ideas contained here. Let them be springboards to other memorable moments for you and your child.

Enjoy the wonder of numbers!

Number Wonder Arts and Crafts

Math and art make a winning combination. This collection of easy and creative art experiences include early math concepts like matching and sorting, patterns, sequence, and order plus number values and recognizing numerals. Children are familiar and at ease with art and they live math everyday; so enjoy bringing the two processes together.

Several art activities are listed below. Each helps to further enhance and strengthen the foundation for basic math principals. Let's start cutting, pasting, counting, and creating!

Jelly Bean Jamboree
Things you'll need:

plastic tray covered with a towel for each child	stickers
clean large plastic jar with lid for each child	markers
large jelly beans, a variety of colors	plain stick-on labels

How To:
1. Pour the large jelly beans on a towel covered tray.
2. Sort the jelly beans by color. Then pair them, count them into groups of five, etc.
3. Sort the jelly beans into the jars.
4. Place the lid on tightly.
5. With markers and stickers decorate the large stick-on labels for each jar. Press the label on the jar.
6. When teaching a specific number get out the jelly bean jars and sort the beans to match the number being taught.

Jammin' Jewels
Things you'll need:
cereal with holes (Cheerios™, Fruit Loops™, Apple Jacks™)
shoe strings, yarn, or heavy twine
masking tape

How To:
1. If you are using yarn or twine, tape the end of the string with masking tape to form a "needle" to use for picking up the cereal.
2. Push the taped end of the yarn through the hole in the cereal. Make a pattern by sorting colors or types of cereals together. (Like 10 red Fruit Loops™, 5 Cheerios™, etc.)
3. When the necklace is full, tie the ends together to form a necklace.

Paper Cup Bingo
Things you'll need:

10 paper cups	markers
wooden board or Styrofoam™	glue
pennies	

How To:
1. Write the numbers 1 to 10 on the paper cups.
2. Glue the paper cups to a wooden or Styrofoam™ board.
3. Give each child 5 pennies and have them toss the pennies into the paper cups.
4. Add the scores to see who has the highest number. The highest score wins all the pennies.

Counting Container

Things you'll need:

container such as a wooden cheese box, hat box, shoe box, or cigar box
paints
glue
number stickers
beads
sponge numbers
colored cellophane
ribbon

How To:

1. Decorate the cheese box and lid with number stickers, paints with number sponges, and beads.
2. Line the inside of the box with the colored cellophane.
3. Fill the container with blocks, number games, and small toys. Use the container to give as a gift.
   *Fill the container with count down dining: one large loaf of bread, 2 jars of preserves, 3 wedges of cheese, 4 plastic glasses, 5 napkins, etc.

Number Collage

Things you'll need:

scissors
magazines
glue
poster board

How To:

1. Have several stacks of magazines to look through to find pictures of numbers. Cut out the pictures of numbers.
2. Cut out large numbers from the poster boards. Match the numbers cut out from the magazines to the large number shapes cut from the poster board.
3. Glue the matching numbers to the poster board number shapes.

Number Wrapping Paper

Things you'll need:
butcher paper
sponge numbers
tempera paints

How To:

1. Place the butcher paper on a covered surface, dip the number sponges in the paints and decorate the butcher paper.
2. Dry thoroughly.

"How Old Am I" Tee Shirt

Things you'll need:

old or new white tee-shirt
big buttons
fabric glue

fabric paint
fabric crayons

How To:

1. Pick an age to celebrate, such as four. (Great activity for a birthday party.)
2. Count and select 4 fancy buttons, glue the buttons to the tee shirt.
3. Decorate the shirt with the fabric and crayon paints using the number 4.
4. Add other trims, ribbons, or beads to make the tee shirt special, yet still washable.

Rice Paintings

Things you'll need:

dark sheet of matte paper
glue

How To:

1. Draw a number on the matte board with a squeeze bottle of white glue, before the glue dries place the matte board face down into the rice.
2. Using your hands pour handfuls of rice over the number until the glue dries.

Dot Sticker Chains

Things you'll need:

Heavy twine
round colored stickers
markers

large cookie sheet with sides
rice

How To:

1. Measure 3 feet of twine for each child.
2. Stick the stickers together 2 by 2.
3. Write the numbers on the stickers and you have a long counting garland.

Number Rock Garden

Things you'll need:

aluminum muffin tin
tempera paints
paintbrushes
empty yogurt cups or small
    milk cartons to mix paint in

white glue
small rocks and stones, cleaned and dried
butcher paper or newspaper to cover work area

How To:

1. Mix the paint in the yogurt containers.
2. Mix a different color paint in each container, stir with the paintbrush.
3. Paint the rocks different colors and dry.
4. In one section of the muffin tin, glue one rock, in another section glue two rocks, in another section glue three rocks. Glue as many rocks as can be counted.

*You may want to use glitter glue to coat the painted rocks to add sparkle.

Number Tree

Things you'll need:
plastic hanger
twine
large white name tag stickers
markers
buttons
glue
small stickers

How To:
1. Cut enough twine to hold the numbers 1-5 on one side and 5 -10 on the other side.
2. On the white stickers write the numbers 1 through 10.
3. Stick the sticker to the twine, stick a plain sticker to the back of the numbered sticker.
4. On the plain sided sticker glue buttons to match the number on the opposite side. Use small stickers when the numbers get to large to glue buttons.
5. Tie the twine to the bottom of the hanger and hang from a door or the ceiling.

Sucker Count

Things you'll need:
25 to 30 suckers
large index cards
scissors
markers

How To:
1. Using the large index cards cut small slits in the cards to insert the sucker sticks.
2. Number the cards so that the slits correspond with the suckers stuck in them.
3. Think of a special number at the beginning of the game and when you get to that number give each child a sucker. "Number knowledge is sweet."

Calendar Count

Things you'll need:
old calendars
scissors
old hat
candies

How To:
1. Cut up old calendars and toss the numbers in an old hat.
2. Have each child select a number from the hat and count out the matching amounts of candy.
3. Piece the calendar back together by lining up the numbers in the proper order.
*For younger children use the first ten days of the month.

Number Nature Hunt

Things you'll need:
plastic bags
old shopping bag with handles
pennies

How To:
1. Designate 10 items to be found outside such as 3 acorns, 2 dandelions, and 5 small leaves
2. Give each child a bag and go outside and hunt the nature items.
3. The child who finishes first gets a dime counted out in pennies.

Toothpick Tapestries

Things you'll need:
2 boxes colored toothpicks
glue
cardboard or heavy poster board
markers

How To:
1. Cut the boards into smaller pieces so they will be easier to handle.
2. Glue the toothpicks on the boards in the shapes of numbers.
3. On another board glue the counted out version of the number shape you made.
4. Write the number of toothpicks counted out at the bottom of the board.

Raisin Rally

Things you'll need:
A small box of raisins for each child
paper plates
measuring cup

How to:
1. Using a paper plate, have each child count out groups of ten raisins from their little box.
2. Add the groups together and count out how many total raisins.
3. Once they have all been counted, pour some of the boxes of raisins into a measuring cup and guess how many it takes to fill one measuring cup.
   * This can also be done with graham cracker squares, vanilla wafers, or butter crackers. Spread the crackers with peanut butter and stick as many raisins as possible onto the top surface of the cracker without stacking. Count how many raisins would fit on each cracker and eat.

Fragrant Beads
Things you'll need:

shoe strings or elastic strings   dough (recipe follows)
toothpicks

Dough Recipe
Things you'll need:

measuring spoons   stove
measuring cups   flavorings: vanilla, almond, lemon
saucepan   food coloring
medium bowl

Ingredients:

1 cup salt   1 cup cornstarch
1 cup water   2 teaspoons flavoring
1 cup cold water

1. Mix the salt and 1 cup water in a saucepan. Bring to a boil.
2. In a medium bowl, stir one half cup cold water into the cornstarch.
3. Add the cornstarch mixture to the boiling water and stir. Add favorite flavoring.
4. Cook over low heat, stirring until like a pie dough.
5. Remove, turn onto a board, cool, and knead until smooth.
7. For colored dough add food coloring into the dough as you are kneading it.

How to make fragrant beads:
1. Pinch a bit of dough from the dough ball.
2. Roll the piece of dough into a ball or cylinder.
3. Poke a hole into the bead using a tooth pick. Leave the bead on the toothpick to dry, sticking the toothpick with the bead into a ball of play dough to hold it. Turn beads occasionally to keep them from sticking.
4. Dry beads until hard, usually one to two days.
5. Sort the beads into like colors and string the beads onto the shoe string or elastic.
   * Do the beads in your favorite Christmas colors and use as a garland for your tree.

Rub a Dub Dub Number Fun
Things you'll need:

stencils of numbers and shapes precut   crayons without paper
    by an adult from heavy paper   markers
drawing paper   tape

How to:
1. Choose one of the number stencils and place it on your work surface. Choose a shape stencil that has the same number of sides (number 3 and triangle).
2. Place the drawing paper over the shapes, tape the corners of the drawing paper so it will not move.
3. Rub over the entire shape with a crayon used sideways.
4. Remove the tape and write the names of the numbers and shapes at the bottom of the paper.

Counting Garden

Things you'll need:
paper muffin cups
construction paper
markers
crayons
glue

How to:
1. Give each child a large piece of construction paper with a number written at the bottom.
2. Have them count out the corresponding number of muffin cups to match the number on the construction paper.
3. Flatten the muffin papers to resemble flowers and glue the "flowers" onto the construction paper.
4. Once they are glued, draw the stems, leaves and flower pot in the appropriate places.
5. Put the masterpiece gardens in numerical order as each child shows their work. Hang them around the room as a reminder of the counting garden.

The Rock Group

Things you'll need:
flat stones or rocks
water and towels for washing and drying rocks
waterproof paint
paintbrushes
markers
stickers
butcher paper or newspaper
clean pizza box or shoe box

How to:
1. Gather a variety of smooth top flat stones.
2. Wash and dry the stones.
3. Paint the top flat area of each stone with any color. Dry thoroughly.
4. Clean up painting stuff.
5. When the stones have dried, draw and decorate them with permanent markers and stickers. Draw faces, (happy, sad, sleepy), make polka-dots, shapes, or other images.
6. Dry.
7. Sort and count the decorated rocks.
8. Store the decorated stones in a pizza box or shoe box. Decorate the box with happy faces on the tops and sides.

 God saw all that he had made, and it was very good. Genesis 1:31

Thank You God for giving us the ability to create and make fun and interesting things. Thank You for our hands and for our ideas that help to make each project unique, just like we are. Amen.

Songs You Can Count On

Children love music. They love the melody, the rhythm and the words. Music is a wonderful vehicle for learning because it is so natural to children. The following songs are songs to sing about numbers and counting.

Tune of "Row, Row, Row Your Boat"
One, one, one, two, three,
One, two, three, four, five;
One, two, three, four, five, six, seven,
Eight, nine, ten, oh, my!

Tune of "10 Little Indians"
(For the month of January)
One little, two little, three little polar bears,
Four little, five little, six little polar bears,
Seven little, eight little, nine little polar bears,
Ten polar bears in the snow.

February: One little, two little, three little Valentines...10 Valentines for my love.
March: One little, two little three little box kites...10 box kites in the sky.
April: One little, two little, three little raindrops...10 raindrops falling down.
May: One little, two little, three little flowers...10 flowers blooming grow.
June: One little, two little, three little June bugs...10 June bugs fly around.
July: One little, two little, three little fireworks...10 fireworks in the night.
August: One little, two little, three little snow cones...10 snow cones nice and cold.
September: One little, two little, three little falling leaves..10 leaves fall to the ground.
October: One little, two little, three little pumpkins...10 pumpkins in the patch.
November: One little, two little, three little turkeys...10 turkeys saying "gobble".
December: One little, two little, three little Christmas trees...10 Christmas trees so bright.

Tune of "When Johnny Comes Marching Home"

The animals went in two by two,
Hurrah! Hurrah!
The animals went in two by two,
Hurrah! Hurrah!
The animals went in two by two,
The elephant and the kangaroo,
And they all went into the ark,
For to get out of the rain.

Tune of "She'll Be Coming Around the Mountain"

We can all count to 10, yes we can!
We can all count to 10, yes we can!
One, two, three, four, and five,
Six, seven, eight, nine, and ten.
We can all count to 10, yes we can!

 You who are godly, sing with joy to the LORD. It is right for honest people to praise him...Sing a new song to him. Play with skill, and shout with joy. Psalm 33:1, 3.

Dear God, thank You for our voices that can sing both counting songs and songs of praise. Amen.

Young children are fascinated with, and able to learn, foreign languages very easily. As you master counting in English, introduce a few other languages. Use a map or a globe to show your child where people live who speak the language you are learning.

These languages can help you teach truths much deeper than the numbers one through ten: they can help you illustrate the fact that differences aren't always very deep. Even though the words sound different than ours, they represent the same things. Even though people may look different, we are all God's children.

English

one
two
three
four
five
six
seven
eight
nine
ten

Spanish

uno (oon-o)
dos (dohss)
trace (trayss)
quatro (kwah-tro)
cinco (seen-ko)
seis (sayss)
siete (syay-tay)
ocho (o-cho)
nueve (nway-vay)
diez (dyess)

French

un (we)
deux (duh)
trois (trwah)
quatre (kahtruh)
sinq (sank)
six (sis)
sept (set)
huit (weet)
neuf (nuhf)
dix (deess)

German

eins (eyns)
zwei (tsvy)
drei (dry)
vier (seer)
funf (fuenf)
sechs (zekhs)
sieben (zeeven)
acht (ahkht)
neun (noyn)
zehn (tsehn)

Swahili (an East African language)

moja (mo-jah)
mbili (m-bee-lee)
tatu (ta-too)
nne (n-nay)
tano (tah-no)
sita (see-tah)
saba (sah-bah)
nane (nah-nay)
tisa (tee-sah)
kuma (koo-mee)

Italian

uno (oon)
due (doo)
tre (tray)
quattro (kwaht-tro)
cinque (cheen-kway)
sei (seh-ee)
sette (set-tay)
otto (o-to)
nove (naw-vay)
dieci (dyeh-chee)

Hebrew

echad (ah-aht)
schnayim (shtah-yeem)
schloschah (shah-yeem)
arba (are-bah)
chamischah (hah-maysh)
schischah (shaysh)
schivah (sheh-vah)
schmonah (shmoe-neh)
tischah (tay-shah)
asarah (eh-sair)

 Suppose I speak in the languages of human beings and of angels. If I don't have love, I am only a loud gong or a noisy cymbal. 1 Corinthians 13:1
Dear God, help me to remember that my words are not as important as my actions. Help me show love to those around me because love is a language everybody understands.

ACTIVITY PAGES FOR NUMBERS 1-12

 1 ONE 1 ONE 1 ONE 1 ONE 1 ONE 1 ONE 1 ONE 1 ONE 1 ONE 1

Directions: draw your face in the circle below. Draw your eyes, your nose, your mouth, your hair, your ears...anything you want to show the special person God made when He made you!

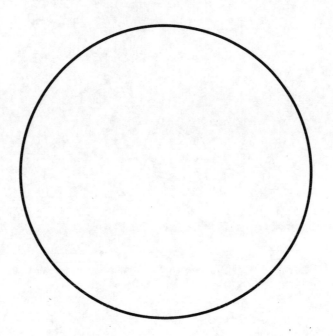

Practice writing the number 1.

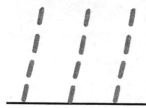

Draw a circle.

Directions: circle the one mirror you like the best. Draw your face inside it.

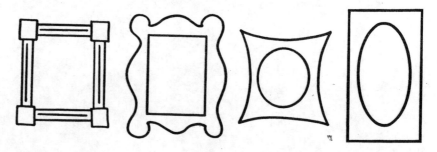

Directions: Draw a line from each animal to its mate.

Practice writing the number 2.

Draw 2 snakes.

41

Directions: Color or decorate three hearts

Practice writing the number 3.

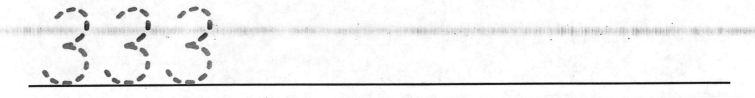

Draw three triangles.

Directions: Cut out the squares along the black lines. Glue or tape them onto the men in the correct order. (Note to Teacher: See Devotion for Number Four on page 37.)

[4]

[1]

[3]

[2]

Practice writing the number 4.

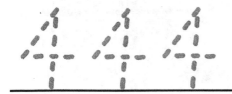

Draw four squares.

Directions: Draw a line from the water pot to the stem with the matching number of grapes on it.

Practice writing the number 6.

Directions: Write the number of jewels each goblet has on the line to the right.

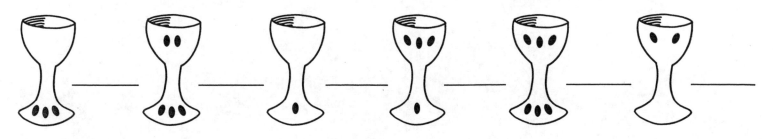

Directions: Count the items in each row and write the number that tells how many are in the row at the end of the line.

Practice writing the number 7.

Directions: Fill in the missing numbers on the scroll.

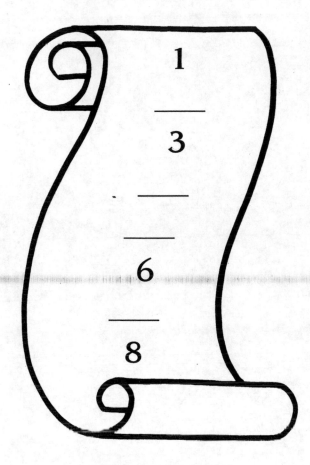

1
__
3
__
__
6
__
8

Practicing writing the number 8.

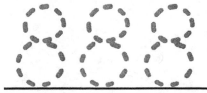

Directions: Draw eight jewels on King Josiah's crown.

Directions: Connect the dots to help the man get back to Jesus to tell Him "Thank you!" (Note to Teacher: See Devotion for Number Nine on page 39.)

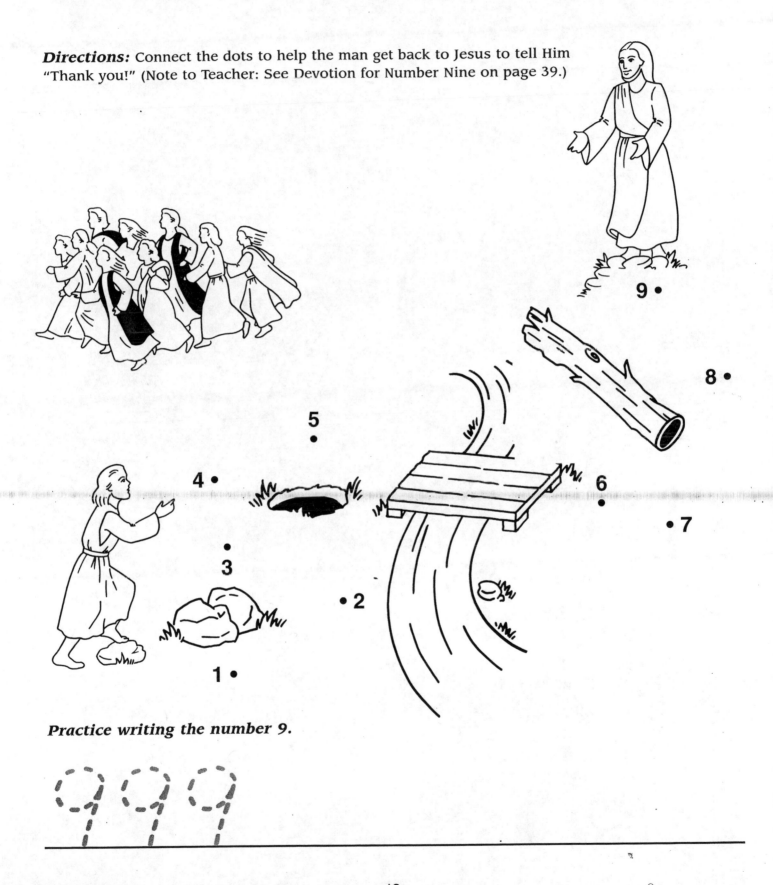

Practice writing the number 9.

Directions: Oh no! The woman has spilled all ten coins this time. Can you help her find the coins? Circle or draw an X on each coin ⊙ you find. Did you find all ten? (Note to Teacher: See Devotion for Number Ten on page 39.)

Practice writing the number 10.

Directions: Circle 10 coins.

Directions: Write in the missing numbers on Joseph's brothers. (Note to Teacher: See Devotion for Number Eleven on page 39.)

Practice writing the number 11.

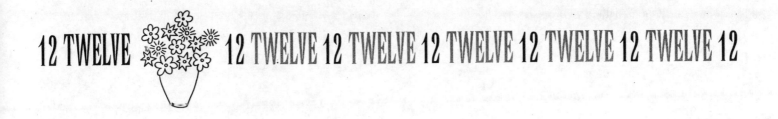
Directions: Which box of lollipops should Sarah buy if she wants to give each of her 12 friends a lollipop? Draw a circle around that box.

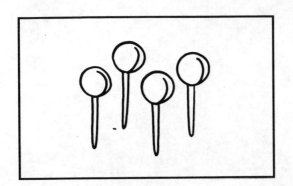

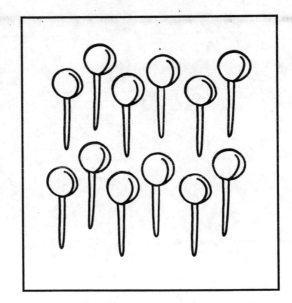

Practice writing the number 12.

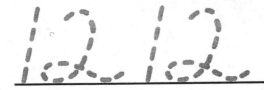

Counting at Home and in Your Neighborhood

Opportunities to count and discover numbers are all around you every day. It isn't necessary to have a formal "lesson" to reinforce the number skills you are teaching your child. In fact, when children learn that math is a part of their world in a casual way, the subject becomes much less threatening. Ideas for having number fun around the house, in your neighborhood, and around your community are included below. This list is just a sample of ideas. . .once you get started, you'll be counting on fun everywhere you go!

Counting Around the House

Toys

Blocks. Build a block city. Since cities have many buildings in many sizes, build towers of differing heights. Build a building with just one block. Next, use two blocks, then three. How many buildings can you build with each one taller than the one before? How many blocks are in your building that has the most blocks?

Balls. How many balls do you have? How many large balls? How many small balls? How many purple balls? How many blue ones? How many times can you catch the ball? How many times can you bounce the ball?

Stuffed Animals. Count your stuffed animals. How many are there? Group your animals into two or more different groups: all bears, all jungle animals, all farm animals, all brown animals, all white animals...you decide the groups. How many groups did you make? How many animals are in each group?

Bath Toys. How many boats in your bath? How many toys go in the tub with you? How many toys float? Can you group them into groups that are alike? How many groups can you make? How many toys are in each group?

Magnets. Magnetic numbers (and letters) make your refrigerator an instant lesson. Find all the fives (or the b's). How many are there? Can you put the numbers in order from 1 to 9? Can you find all the red numbers (or letters)? How many are there? How many blue letters?

House Count

People. How many people live in your house? How many are boys? How many are girls?

Windows. Count the windows in one room. Count the windows in each room and compare: which room has the most? Which room has the least? How many windows in your house?

Clocks. How many clocks are in your house? How many have faces and hands and how many have just numbers? Which kind do you have more of?

Books. How many books are on your shelf? How many books are on the table? How many books have animal pictures in them? How many books have green covers?

Videos. How many videos do you have? How many videos about animals? How many about...?

Helping with the Chores

Time to Eat. How many chairs are at your table? How many plates do you need to set? How many forks will you need? How many spoons? How many napkins? (Making sure each person gets one item is good practice for one-to-one correspondence.)

Taking Out the Trash. How many wastebaskets are in your house? How many trash bags get carried out?

Mail. How many envelopes are you going to mail? How many stamps do you need? Put a stamp on each envelope. How many letters did the mail carrier bring?

Laundry. How many socks? Match the socks. How many towels? How many washcloths? How many pairs of jeans? How many shirts?

15

In Your Backyard and the Neighborhood

Sandbox. How many towers can you make in your sand castle? How many toy trucks can load sand in your sandbox? How many shovels do you have?

Swing set. How many swings on the swing set? How many places for children to sit? How many children are playing?

Slide. How many steps on the ladder?

Sidewalks. How many steps from your door to the sidewalk? How many squares on the sidewalk in front of your home? How many steps to your neighbor's home?

Sidewalk chalk is a wonderful way to draw extra large numbers or pictures for counting. You can also use sidewalk chalk to divide the squares in a sidewalk into pieces. How many pieces do you get when you draw one straight line? How many pieces do you get when you draw two straight lines? How many pieces do you get when you use three straight lines? Can you get a different number if you angle the lines differently?

Houses. How many houses are on your street? How many floors are in your building?

Plants. How many bushes are in front of your house? How many flowers are blooming on a plant? How many different colors of flowers can you find in your yard? On a walk around the neighborhood?

Running Errands Around Your Community

Grocery Store. The grocery store is so full of math lessons that it is impossible to list all the possibilities here. A few ideas can help you get started: Count the apples (peaches, tomatoes, etc.). Find all the 7's (8's, 9's...). Count the cans. Which price is higher? How many kinds of apples do they have? How many shoppers can you count? How many carts do you see? How many eggs in a carton? How many lobsters in the tank? How many magazines by the cash register? Count the items as they're checked out. How many did you buy? When you get home with your purchases, you can count the number of items in a bag!

Shopping. All the same suggestions apply to other stores, just omit the food and, in some cases, the carts. Count the colors of sweaters or shirts. Count other objects in the store. Look for numbers.

Bank. How many lanes in the drive-through? How many tellers at the windows? How many people are in the bank? How many chairs do you see? How many cars are in the drive-through lanes? How many coins did you get?

Gas Station. How many pumps? How many cars do you see? Do you see any numbers? Which numbers do you see? Can you find a 9 (5,3...)?

Waiting Rooms. Waiting for appointments at doctor's offices, garages, or anywhere else is not easy for little ones. Pass the time by counting people, magazines, cars, trucks, or buses that pass by, windows, chairs, workers, pictures on the walls, tables, buttons for soda or food on vending machines. Look for numbers all around the room or outside the window.

At Church

How many cribs in the nursery?
How many steps on the staircase?
How many doors? How many windows?
Look for page numbers in the hymnal.
How many cars in the parking lot? How many white cars?

Eating Out

How many items do you order? How many workers do you see? How many cars in the drive-through line? How many tables in the room? How many chairs at your table? How many people do you see? How many item on the menu? How many french fries in your bag? How many bites to finish your hamburger? How many chicken strips on your plate? How many vegetables? How many pieces of fruit? How many items in the bag? What numbers do you see?

Anywhere, Anytime, Out and About

How many trucks, school buses, red cars, etc. do you see on the way to the ....
How many fire trucks are parked in the fire station?
How many stop signs/lights on your way to .....?
How many "For Sale" signs do you see on the way to...
What numbers do you see in the elevator?
Look for numbers on trucks, taxis, house, or business numbers.
Look for dates on cornerstones and monuments.
Look for simple shapes such as squares, circles, and triangles. Talk about how many sides each shape has. Count how many shapes you find. Clocks, cookies, plates, bottoms of cups...all can be circles found in the kitchen. Manhole covers, streetlights, stoplights, and headlights are circles you might find while out driving.

Teach us to number our days aright, that we may gain a heart of wisdom.
Psalm 90:12   *Scripture taken from the HOLY BIBLE, NEW INTERNATIONAL VERSION. Copyright © 1973, 1978, 1984 International Bible Society. Used by permission Zondervan Bible Publishers. All rights reserved.*

Dear God, You have made a world full of wonderful things to enjoy and to count. You have given us wonderful days to enjoy them. Thank You for each day that I have in Your world. Amen.

Books to Count On

Math isn't just about number skills. Verbal skills have also been shown to help children succeed in mathematics. Reading to your children is not just one of the best ways to prepare your children for success in reading. A rich vocabulary will also help your children understand directions, explain why a math problem is solved as it is, and comprehend story problems. The following books feature number concepts. Look for them and others like them at your library or bookstore and add them to your story time so that your children don't feel math is an isolated category for numbers only.

Alda, Arlene. *Sheep, Sheep, Sheep, Help Me Fall Asleep*. A Doubleday Book for Young Readers, 1992.

While fighting sleep, the narrator resists mother's suggestion to count sheep by imagining other animals doing silly things. Eventually, drowsiness wins out and the narrator "sees" an increasing number of sheep--from one to ten. No numerals here but lovely photographs and accompanying stars to match the number of sheep pictured on each page.

Anno, Mitsumasa. *Anno's Counting Book*. Thomas Y. Crowell Company, 1977.

Introduces counting and number systems by showing mathematical relationships in nature. A beautiful wordless book with several concepts included in each illustration.

Ashton, Elizabeth Allen. *An Old-Fashioned 123 Book*. Viking, 1991.

A counting book featuring art work from turn-of-the-century illustrator Jessie Wilcox Smith. Each two-page spread features an elaborate numeral and four-line verse on the left with an old-fashioned illustration on the right.

Astley, Judy. *When One Cat Woke Up*. Dial Books for Young Readers, 1990.

From stealing two fish to leaving ten muddy paw prints, the cat romps through the house as the numbers one through ten are illustrated.

Bang, Molly. *Ten, Nine, Eight*. Greenwillow Books, 1983.

A countdown to bedtime begins with "10 small toes all washed and warm" and ends with "1 big girl all ready for bed." Large numerals appear in the text.

Bridwell, Norman. *Clifford Counts Bubbles*. Scholastic Trade, 1992.

The red puppy named Clifford learns about playing with bubbles in a chunky-shaped board book that focuses on toddlers' experiences.

Brooks, Alan. *Frogs Jump*. Scholastic Trade, 1996.

A counting book illustrated by Steven Kellogg. Silly animals count from 1 to 12 and back again.

Calmenson, Stephanie. *Dinner at the Panda Palace*. HarperCollins Publisher, 1991.

The Panda Palace restaurant opens as parties of animals from one to ten arrive looking for tables.

Crews, Donald. *Ten Black Dots*. Greenwillow Books, 1968, 1986.

"What can you do with ten black dots?" Count to ten with graphic illustrations of simple rhymes such as "Two dots can make the eyes of a fox."

Crews, Donald. *Bicycle Race*. Greenwillow Books, 1985.

Twelve bicyclists compete in a race wearing numbered helmets. Follow the bicyclists by keeping track of the numerals on their helmets.

Dunham, Meredith, Lothrop and Lee. *Numbers: How Do You Say It?* Shepard Books, 1990.

Numbers in four languages with graphic drawings and each number on the page.

Ehlert, Lois. *Fish Eyes*. Voyager Books, 1990.

A counting book depicting the colorful fish a child might see if he turned into a fish himself.

Falwell, Cathryn. *Feast for 10*. Clarion Books, 1993.

What does it take to make a feast for 10 hungry people? Start with one shopping cart, two pumpkins, three chickens. In rhymed text, count to 10 once in the grocery store as the children help Mama shop, and again at home as everyone lends a hand to prepare the meal.

Feelings, Muriel. *Moja Means One*. Dial Books for Young Readers, 1971. (Caldecott Honor Book).

A Swahili counting book uses the numeral, the Swahili number word (pronunciation guide included), and an illustration of some aspect of East African life to teach counting from one to ten.

Fleming, Denise. *Count!* Henry Holt & Co., 1992.

Wiggle like a worm, bounce like a kangaroo, leap like a frog! Count from one gnu to 10 lizards to 50 bees.

Giganti, Paul. *Each Orange Had Eight Slices: A Counting Book Vol. 1*. Greenwillow, 1992.

Introduces beginning math concept with dynamic illustrations and appealing words that combine in a book that can be shared by youngsters and adults.

Greenfield, Eloise. *Aaron and Gayla's Counting Book*. Writers & Readers, 1994.

Text helps children count from 1 to 20 and is accompanied by illustrations of Aaron and Gayla playing outside on a rainy day.

Halsey, Megan. *3 Pandas Planting*. Simon & Schuester, 1994.

From 12 crocodiles car pooling to 3 pandas planting to 1 elephant enjoying the earth, this counting book brings ecology to the preschool level.

Hill, Eric. *Spot's First Easter*. Penguin, 1991.

A flap book in which the Easter bunny has hidden some eggs for Spot and his friend, Helen, to find. The search for the eggs becomes a counting game.

Johnston, Tony. *Whale Song*. G. P. Putnam's Sons, 1987.

A story suggesting that the songs exchanged by the giant creatures is really just counting from one to ten.

Kitchen, Bert. *Animal Numbers*. Dial Books, 1987.

A counting book in which animals both exotic and familiar are shown with the specified number of infants. The animals are shown on, in and around large numerals. (No text)

Mazzola, Frank. *Counting Feathers*. Charlesbridge, 1997.

As a cat waits patiently, birds from one to twenty land at a feeder. Includes information about the various species and the seeds they eat.

MacDonald, Suse and Bill Oakes. _Numblers_. Dial Books for Young Readers, 1988.
On each double-page spread a number from one to ten changes gradually into a familiar object or animal, splitting apart in the process into the appropriate number of parts or pieces. (Descriptive text in the back gives clues to the nature of the thing depicted.)

Mack, Stan. _10 Bears in My Bed_. Pantheon Books, 1974.
A variation of the familiar goodnight countdown as the bears leave the bed one by one by skating, roaring, etc. as they go.

McGrath, Barbieri. _M and M's Counting Book_. Charlesbridge, 1994.
A book of activities to do with the brightly colored candies. Brightly colored illustrations on each page demonstrate the activities.

McMillan, Bruce. _Counting Wildflowers_. Lothrop, Lee & Shepard Books, 1986.
A counting book with photographs of wildflowers illustrating the numbers one through twenty.

Medearis, Angel Shelf. _Picking Peas for a Penny_. State House Press, 1990.
A rhythmical, lyrical counting rhyme that's also a biographical poem about the memories of life on a farm during the Depression.

Miller, Jane. _Farm Counting Book_. Prentice-Hall, 1983.
Introduces simple number concepts using color photographs of favorite farm animals.

Murphy, Stuart J. _Every Buddy Counts_. HarperCollins Publishers, 1997.
A little girl goes through the day counting her "buddies" which include one hamster, two sisters, three kittens, etc. Excellent suggestions are given at the back for further exploration of math concepts. This book is one of a series called MathStart.

Nikola-Lisa, W. _1, 2, 3, Thanksgiving!_ Albert Whitman & Co., 1991.
A Thanksgiving counting book depicting the numbers 1 through 10 through scenes of the holiday.

Oakes, Bill and Suse MacDonald. _Puzzlers._ Dial books for Young Readers, 1989.
An introduction to concepts such as "widest," "tallest," and "back-to-back" where the reader is asked to pick out the number with that quality in an animal that is made up of numbers. A more advanced book but answers are included.

Owens, Mary Beth. _Counting Cranes Vol. 1_. Little Brown & Co., 1993.
Delicate watercolor paintings and a haiku-like text are in this counting book that describes the characteristics and behavior of the whooping crane.

Pittman, Helena Clare. _Counting Jennie_. Carolrhoda Books, 1993.
From her sister's scarves and her mother's shoes to her brother's hats and her father's ties, Jennie counts everything she sees and young readers count along with Jennie on an eventful bus ride to school.

Seiden, Art. _Baby's 1-2-3: A Counting Song (So Tall Board Book)_. Grosset & Dunlap, 1992.
From the mother turtle and her little turtle "one" to the mother firefly and her little flies "ten," small children will love to count the baby animals in this variation of a familiar children's song.

Sierra, Judy. _Counting Crocodiles_. Harcourt Brace Jovanovich, 1997.
In this rhymed retelling of a traditional Asian tale, a clever monkey uses her ability to count to outwit the hungry crocodiles that stand between her and a banana tree on another island across the sea.

Smith, Maggie. *Counting Our Way to Maine*. Orchard Books, 1995.
On a trip to Maine, the family counts from one baby to twenty fireflies.

Spencer, Eve. *Animal Babies 1 2 3 (Ready Set Read)*. Raintree/Steck Vaughn, 1990.
Numbers from 1 to 10 are illustrated with different baby animals and information is provided about their traits and habits.

Szekeres, Cyndy. *Cyndy Szekeres' Teeny Mouse Counts Herself*. Golden Press, 1992.
At bedtime, Teeny Mouse counts her eyes, her teeth, her furry paws and wiggly toes, the buttons on her nightgown and the ribbons in her hair--and falls asleep by the time she gets to 10.

Tabor, Nancy Maria Grande. *A Taste of the Mexican Market/El Gusto del Mercado Mexicano*. Charlesbridge Publishing.
A book written in both Spanish and English, it takes readers of all ages on a trip to a colorful Mexican market to learn the names of fruits and vegetables in two languages and to play a counting game.

Tabor, Nancy Maria Grande. *Cicuenta En La Cebra: Contando con Los Animales/Fifty on the Zebra: Counting with the Animals (Bilingual Books)*. Charlesbridge Publishing, 1995.
This bilingual counting book contains 10 dragons on parade, 11 oysters at the opera, and 18 Dalmatians showing off their diamonds. As they count, readers are asked questions relating to the colorful cut-paper pictures while they review concepts such as color, size, and shape.

Tallarico, Tony. *Counting Picture Book (Preschool Can You Find)*. Grosset & Dunlap, 1992.
Small children search for familiar animals and objects as they learn about numbers in a colorful counting board book.

Tafur, Nancy. *Who's Counting?* Greenwillow Books, 1986.
A curious puppy pads across the fields and through the barnyard and encounters many surprises from one squirrel to five eggs to an unexpected ten. A beautiful and simple book.

Walsh, Ellen Stoll. *Mouse Count*. Harcourt Brace Jovanovich, 1991.
A hungry snake finds ten little mice and counts them into a jar for dinner. Will ten be enough? The snake slips off for one more mouse and while he's gone the mice "uncount" themselves and run away.

Ward, Brenda. *Counting on Angels*. Compass Books, 1995.
A beautifully illustrated pop-up book with rhymed text.

Yoshi. *1, 2, 3*. Simon & Schuester, 1991.
A cumulative counting tale in which one innocent inchworm precipitates busy activity among an increasing number of animals. Hidden in each picture is a numeral, disguised among the shapes of the natural world.

Blessed is the one who reads the words of this prophecy. Blessed are those who hear it and think everything it says is important. The time when these things will come true is near. Revelation 1:3

Thank You God for Your Bible and the words it has to help us learn about You, about how much You love us, and about how You want us to live. Thank You that we learn as we read. Amen.

Number Wonder Recipes

Kids love to cook! Counting in the kitchen is a wonderful vehicle for teaching and entertaining hungry troops. It reinforces math and language skills, and it encourages organization and sequential thinking.

Number Wonder recipes gives you a plan for pulling out the pots and pans and mixing together some interesting ways to count. The best news of all is that you end up with edible numbers and countable cakes to taste, try, and share.

Decide on the math idea you want to convey, read the suggested recipe, plan ahead and have all the ingredients on hand. Any preparation that needs to be done by you can be done ahead which will help the preparation be more enjoyable for everyone. Happy Cooking!

"Give Me Five" Cookies   Makes 6 to 8 hands depending on size

Things you'll need:

plastic wrap	table knife	scissors
wax paper	cookie sheet	rolling pin
pencil or marker	construction paper	spatula

Ingredients:

1 to 2 tubes of prepared cookie dough	1/4 cup powdered sugar
tube icing	licorice
sprinkles	silver balls

1. Chill dough thoroughly. While the dough is chilling trace around your hand on some heavy construction paper. Cut out your hand shape with a pair of scissors.
2. When the prepared dough has thoroughly chilled, place it on a sheet of wax paper. Roll it out to a thickness of about 1/4 inch, using a rolling pin coated with powdered sugar.
3. Place your hand pattern on the dough and cut around the pattern with a plastic knife. Carefully remove the hand shape with a spatula and place it on a cookie sheet.
4. Bake for 10 to 12 minutes in a 350 degree oven until golden brown.
5. Decorate your hand cookies with icing and sprinkle with favorite candies.
   *Make a watch, ring or bracelet out of the candies for a fancy finish.

Number Wonder Cookies   Makes 24 cookies

Things you'll need:

cutting board	number cookie cutters
cookie sheet	pastry brush
measuring cups	2 small bowls

Ingredients:

6 large flour tortillas	1 cup (1 stick) butter, melted
1/4 cup sugar	1 tablespoon cinnamon

1. Preheat oven to 350 degrees.
2. Place tortillas on a cutting board and cut with number shape cookie cutters. Place on a cookie sheet.
3. Brush the melted butter generously on the tortillas with a pastry brush. (Do this step quickly so that the tortillas do not curl up and harden)
4. In a small bowl combine the sugar and cinnamon, stir thoroughly.
5. Sprinkle the sugar cinnamon mixture over the tortillas.
6. Place in the oven and bake for eight to ten minutes.
 * To color the sugar put it in a jar mix it with a few drops of food coloring and shake thoroughly to combine.

Two By Two Noah Sandwiches   Makes 25 sandwiches

Things you'll need:
measuring cups
cutting board
knife

Ingredients:
50 animal crackers
1/4 cup strawberry cream cheese
1/4 cup bananas, thinly sliced

1. Group animal crackers in pairs.
2. Spread the flat side of one animal cracker with the flavored cream cheese.
   (When you pair the animal crackers, place them going in the same direction, one side of the sandwich will have the flat side of the cracker out.)
3. Top the cream cheese with the sliced banana and then with the second animal cookie.

Counting Kabobs   Makes 4 kabobs

Things you'll need:
knife
4 ten-inch wooden skewers
cutting board

Ingredients
2 1-inch deli slices of turkey, cubed
8 mini muffins
8 1-inch cubes of cheese
8 large grapes

1. Alternate ingredients on each skewer in the same order: turkey cube, grape, cheese, mini-muffin.
2. Continue this process until the skewer is full.

Domino Cookies

Things you'll need:
wax paper
plates

Ingredients:
1 package chocolate wafer cookies
white tube frosting

1. Place the wafer cookies on a plate.
2. Using a pointed tip, squirt dots on the cookies to resemble dominos.

Bread Baton Numbers

Things You'll Need:

large bowl

measuring cups

wax paper

grater

knife

2 forks or pastry blender

measuring spoons

cookie sheet

rolling pin

Ingredients:

2 1/4 cups flour

1 cup water

1 cup Cheddar cheese, grated

2 1/4 sticks butter, cut into small pieces

1 tablespoon salt

1. Combine the flour and butter in a large bowl, using 2 forks or a pastry blender. Cut the butter until the mixture resembles coarse bread crumbs.
2. Add the water and salt and mix until a soft dough forms. Form into a ball, wrap in wax paper, and chill one hour.
3. Preheat the oven to 400 degrees. Lightly grease a cookie sheet and set aside.
4. Grate cheese. Lightly flour a smooth surface and sprinkle with cheese.
5. Roll out the chilled pastry on the flour-cheese surface to form a square, about 1/4-inch thick. Cut the batons into strips about six to eight inches long and 1/2-inch wide.
6. Shape the batons into numbers and bake for about 10 minutes or until puffed and golden.

Counting Cupcakes

Things you'll need:

large bowl

electric mixer

jelly roll pan

cooling rack

measuring cups

3 medium bowls

wax paper

star-shaped cookie cutters

measuring spoons

spoons

knife or wooden skewer

Ingredients:

1 box white cake mix

blue food coloring

red cinnamon candies or mini candied chocolate candies

red food coloring

white canned frosting

1. Preheat the oven to 350 degrees.
2. Prepare the cake mix according to the package directions.
3. Divide the batter into thirds and place in three separate bowls. To one bowl add one to two teaspoons red food coloring and mix well. Add blue food coloring to the batter in the second bowl, and leave the batter in the third bowl white. (Use whatever colors you want to show 3 colors after baking)
4. Line a jelly-roll pan with wax paper. Spoon the three batters into the jelly roll pan in a checker board fashion. Swirl with a knife or wooden skewer.
5. Bake for 15 to 20 minutes, or until the wooden pick inserted into the middle comes out clean. Remove from the oven and cool on a cooling rack.
6. Cut the cooled cake with the star shaped cookie cutters.
7. Ice the middle of the cakes and count out the red cinnamon candies or mini chocolate candies to go on each cake.

3 Corner Hat Cookies   Makes 2 dozen cookies

Things you'll need:

2 medium bowls	measuring cups	measuring spoons
electric mixer	plastic wrap	knife
cookie sheet		

Ingredients:

1 cup shortening	1/4 cup oil	3/4 cup sugar
1 cup orange juice	2 teaspoons vanilla extract	3 cups all-purpose flour
2 teaspoons baking powder	pinch of salt	1 cup orange marmalade

1. Cream the shortening, oil, sugar, orange juice, and vanilla extract in a medium bowl.
2. In a separate bowl, stir together flour, baking powder, and salt, then add shortening mixture; stir thoroughly to combine.
3. Form the dough into 2 cylinders and wrap in plastic wrap. Refrigerate until firm.
4. Preheat oven to 350 degrees.
5. Cut 3/8-inch slices from the chilled dough and place on a cookie sheet. Pinch the round piece of dough on the top and sides to form a triangle shape.
6. Place 1 teaspoon orange marmalade in the center of each triangle.
7. Bake for 15 minutes, or until the edges are lightly brown.

Edible Sculptures

Things you'll need:

flat 11 X 7 Styrofoam™ block	colored plastic wrap
masking tape	assorted fruits, washed and cut
large bowl	paper plates
colored toothpicks	

Ingredients:

1. Cover the Styrofoam™ block with the colored plastic wrap. Tape the loose edges onto the bottom of the Styrofoam™. This will be the base for the sculptures.
2. Place the fruits in a large bowl.
3. Select the fruit pieces and place on the toothpicks.
4. Assemble the fruit pieces in order or in any design and stick into the Styrofoam™ base.
   *arrangement suggestion: small to large, soft to crisp

Marshmallow Madness

Things you'll need:

plastic knifes	paper plates

Ingredients:

graham crackers	peanut butter
chocolate squares	mini marshmallows

1. Spread half of a graham cracker with peanut butter, top with a chocolate square.
2. Give each child a number and ask them to place the correct amount of mini-marshmallows onto the chocolate square.
3. Top the marshmallows with the second half of the graham cracker. (If a microwave is available, microwave for 20 to 30 seconds, cool and serve.)

10 Commandment Salad

Things you'll need:

large bowl   cutting board
knife   spoon
small paper cups for serving   plastic spoons

Ingredients: *(You select the amounts and teach measuring with this recipe)*

Mandarin oranges   grapes
bananas   pears
strawberries   raspberries
blueberries   kiwi
apples   mini marshmallows

1. Combine all the above ingredients in a large bowl, stir to combine.

Munch A Bunch Number Crunch

Things you'll need:

oven   large wooden spoon
measuring cups and spoons   large baking pan

Ingredients:
1/4 cup butter, melted
1 cup brown sugar

Start counting with:

10 tablespoons square wheat cereal   5 tablespoons dried bananas
9 tablespoons goldfish pretzels   4 tablespoons milk chocolate chips
8 tablespoons almonds   3 tablespoons sunflower seeds
7 tablespoons raisins   2 tablespoons golden raisins
6 tablespoons dried apricots   1 cup prepared granola

1. Mix all the ingredients in a large baking pan, stir to combine.
2. Bake in a 350 degree oven for 5 to 6 minutes. Remove and stir thoroughly.
3. Cool. Store in an airtight container.

Freezing Fours Number Sundae

Things you'll need:

bowls and spoons   knife to cut the ice cream
measuring cup   small bowls for ingredients

Ingredients:
1 half gallon block of vanilla ice cream
1 cup each small fruits, small cookies, animal crackers, sprinkles

1. Remove the paper container from the ice cream block.
2. Divide the ice cream block into individual slices with a knife (adult helper).
3. Place the ice cream blocks into each individual bowl, as a canvas for a budding artist.
4. Count each different ingredient that will be used to decorate the number sundae and decorate the ice cream block.

Wiggle Waggle Number Fun

Things you'll need:

2 13 X 9 baking pans   measuring cups
spoons   knife
bowls   spoons

Ingredients:

2 large (6 ounce) packages gelatin
2 cups mandarin orange, grapes, cherries, or other favorite fruits

1. Prepare one of the gelatin boxes according to package directions, do not put fruit in this one.
2. Prepare the second box of gelatin according to package directions adding the fruit.
3. Place the gelatin into the refrigerator to congeal.
4. When congealed cut the plain gelatin into countable cubes.
5. When the fruited gelatin has congealed cut it into cubes also.
   *Use the fruited one to count the pieces of fruit in each gelatin cube.
   *If you have number cookie cutters use them to cut out number shapes to go into the gelatin salad.

Polka-Dot Marshmallow Design

Things you'll need:

food coloring in cups thinned by using a little water   small, clean paintbrushes
wax paper or butcher paper for the work surface   pointed wooden sticks (skewers)
masking tape
block of Styrofoam™ covered with colored plastic wrap for the base

Ingredients:

2 bags of large white marshmallows
several bags of mini candies to use to cover the base of the sculpture
white tube icing

1. Cover the Styrofoam™ with the colored plastic wrap, use the masking tape to secure the plastic on the opposite side.
2. Spread the marshmallows on the wax paper covered surface.
3. Paint the marshmallows with the skewers, using polka dots, circles or other shapes that you can count. (While the marshmallows are drying decorate the base of the sculpture with the small candies, using the white tube icing as glue.)
4. Dry the painted marshmallow, when dry press the marshmallow onto the flat end of the skewer, press the pointed end of the skewer into the plastic covered Styrofoam™.
   *Add marshmallows to the sticks, sideways, and in all directions to form a sculpture.

Peanut Butter Play Dough Numbers

Things you'll need:

bowl, spoons

Ingredients:

2 cups non-fat powdered milk   2 cups peanut butter
1 cup honey

1. Mix together until a soft pliable dough is formed.
2. Divide the play dough into individual servings and have each child form a number.

Teddy Bear Tea

Things you'll need:

A menu: Teddy Grahams™, string cheese, Gummy Bears™, Ritz Bits™, blueberries
guests to count
cups and saucers
spoons
napkins
plates
small bowls
small sacks for packing
markers

Ingredients:

Punch (tea)
Plate of counted goodies
To-Go goodie bags (for Daddy or siblings)

1. Count out 5 small bowls, fill the bowls with each of the ingredients for the Teddy Bear Tea. (Count out the ingredients into each bowl.)
2. Count out the plates for everyone at the tea, do the same with spoons, cups and saucers and napkins.
3. Write numbers 1-10 on the paper sack, to decorate the sack.
4. Count out the tea ingredients into the sack.

Fruited Ice Cubes

Things you'll need:
ice cube trays
water pitcher

Ingredients:
100% fruit juice
raspberries

1. Pour the fruit juice into a pitcher and pour into the ice cube trays.
2. Count raspberries from 1 to 3 into each individual ice tray section.
3. Place the filled ice cube tray into the freezer.

I am giving you every plant on the face of the whole earth that bears its own seeds. I am giving you every tree that has fruit with seeds in it. All of them will be given to you for food. Genesis 1:29

Thank You God for providing delicious foods that gives us strength so we can tell our friends about You. Your gifts to us are wonderful; Your plans for our lives is perfect. Thank You God for Your awesome love.

"Game" and "fun" are words that often seem synonymous. But old-fashioned card or board games can also be much more than fun: they are engaging and interactive learning experiences. Unlike educational computer programs or educational TV shows, games can create wonderful memories for your children when you join them for the game.

Several games are described and listed below. They reinforce concepts that are important to establishing the strong foundation children need to learn more advanced math concepts later. You'll find some old favorites and some new names.

Young children are usually not concerned about, and often do not understand, "winning" and "losing". Just enjoy learning and playing without any emphasis on the competition at this point. If more than one child is playing, be sure to encourage everyone to celebrate each players' accomplishments.

Concentration (also known as "Memory")
Number of Players: 1 or 2

Determine the size of the game you want to try with your child by selecting the number of pairs or "matches" your child will find. Very little ones should only have three pairs, perhaps two twos, two threes, and two fours. Older children may want to find matches for the entire deck. Experiment to find a level that challenges without creating frustration.

Shuffle the cards. Deal them all out face down. It helps to place the cards in a kind of grid, such as two rows of three.

The first player turns two cards face up. If the cards' numbers (or values) match, the player keeps the cards and takes another turn. If the pair doesn't match, the player turns the cards face down and the next person plays.

This is an incredibly easy but worthwhile game. You can make your own set of cards using 3" x 5" index cards. Your cards may match the numerals one to ten (or higher) or match a numeral with a picture grouping of that number of items, such as the numeral 4 with a card showing four truck stickers.

Alternative: Using the insert in the middle of this book, cut out the number cards and place them face down. Play the game as described above.

Crazy Eights
Number of Players: 2 or more

"Crazy Eights" is a game for children who are five years of age or older or are already very familiar with the cards. Players must work with both the cards' numbers and shapes (suits) in order to play this game.

Seven cards are dealt to each player. The remaining cards are placed face down to form a draw pile in the middle of the table. The top card is turned over and placed face up next to the draw pile in order to form a discard pile.

Players may look at their cards but should try not to let the others see them. The youngest player must place a card face up on the discard pile. The card must either be the same number (six or queen) or the same shape (spade, diamond, heart, or club) as the card already showing on the discard pile. However, eights are wild and may be discarded at any time regardless of the number or shape showing on the discard pile. When discarding an eight, the player who plays it must announce his choice of shape (heart, spade, club, or diamond). The next player must play either that shape or another eight.

If the player cannot play a card that matches the number or shape of the discard pile or an eight, she must take a card from the draw pile. If she can play that one, she may; if not, her turn is over. The player to her left continues in the same way.

The winner is the first to play all the cards in his hand.

Happy Families   *Number of Players: 3 or more*

All cards are dealt face down to the players. It does not matter if players do not begin with an equal number of cards. Each player looks at his cards and sorts them into "families". A family is four cards of the same value, such as four fives or four queens. Families are placed on the table in front of the players as they are collected. Players should try not to let the others see their cards.

The youngest player begins the game by asking any other player for a particular card that he wants to help complete a family. She may ask for any individual card she chooses as long as she already has at least one member of that family in her hand. If the player asked has the card then it must be given to the player requesting it who may again ask any other player for any particular card. She can go on doing this for as long as he continues to receive the cards he asks for. When a player is asked for a card he does not have then it becomes his turn to asks other players for the cards he wants.

The game ends when all the cards have been collected into families. The player who has collected the most families is the winner.

Snap   *Number of players: 2 or more*

All cards are dealt out to the players one card at a time and face down. It doesn't matter if players do not have exactly equal numbers of cards. Cards are kept face down in a neat pile in front of each player. Players do not look at the cards. The youngest child takes the top card from his pile and puts it face up on the table to start a new pile next to his face-down pile. The player to the left does the same as do the rest of the players. Only the top card of each face-up pile should be seen.

Whenever any player sees that the cards on top of any two face-up piles have the same value (such as two sevens) she calls "Snap". The first player to do so winds both piles and adds them to the bottom of his own face-down pile. Play then starts again with the player to the left of the last player turning over a card.

A player who has played all the cards from his face-down pile can still stay in the game as long as she still has a face-up pile in front of her. She passes when it is her turn to play a card, but she may still call "Snap" when she sees two cards of the same value, and may then get a new face-down pile. A player is out of the game only when he has neither a face-up nor face-down pile.

If a player calls "Snap" in error when there aren't two cards of the same value showing, then he must give each of the other players a card from the bottom of his face-down pile. These cards are added to the bottom of the other players' face-down piles. The winner is the player who wins all the cards.

Camping

This game is known by many names and has many variations. It is played by two or more people, requires no equipment and is a good game for little ones. The first player says, "I went camping and I took one _____" and fills in one item taken. The next player repeats what has already been said and adds two of something else to the list. Play continues with each player adding the next highest number of something added to the camping trip. For example, Player A says, "I went camping and I took one tent." Player B would then say, "I went camping and I took one tent and two flashlights." Player C or Player A would then say, "I went camping and I took one tent, two flashlights and three..." Variations include "I went shopping and I bought..." or " I went to the moon and I took ..." , etc.

War Number of players: 2

"War" is the game to introduce to the youngest children. It is the easiest to learn and the easiest to play.

Remove face cards from the deck. (This step may be omitted if you want to teach the increasing value of jacks to kings. However, to reinforce number skills, they're not necessary). All remaining cards are dealt face down to the two players. Players do not look at the cards but put them into neat, face-down piles in front of them. Each player picks up the top card from his pile and the two cards are placed face up and side by side in the middle of the table.

The player who put the card with the highest value on the table wins both of them and puts the cards, face down, at the bottom of his pile. (Decide if you want aces to represent "1" and have the least value or if you want to present them as the highest value before the game begins.)

If both cards are of the same value, each player takes a card from the top of his pile and places it face down on top of her original card. She then plays one more card face up on top of that. If the two top cards are again equal, this process is repeated until one of the two top cards is higher than the other. The player of the higher card wins all the cards in the middle of the table.

This game may be played until one player wins all the cards or stopped at an agreed-upon time limit. The winner is the player with the highest number of cards in a timed game. Little ones can end the game whenever interest ends.

Hopscotch Number of players: 2 through 4

Equipment needed: sidewalk chalk and unique markers such as bean bags or rocks

Draw a diagram such as the one pictured at right on a section of sidewalk. (The diagrams and rules can vary widely in hopscotch games. The classic pattern and game is described here.)

The first player throws her marker onto square 1, then jumps into 2 on one foot. She then hops on one foot to square 3, then to 4 and 5 at once, landing with one foot in each. Next, she lands with one foot in 6, then two feet in 7 and 8, followed by two feet in 9 and 10 at the same time. Now she jumps up into the air, turns halfway around, reversing the position of her feet. She then hops back to square 1 the same way. Before jumping into square 1, she picks up her marker, then jumps into 1 and hops out of the diagram. (Players may not land in any square that holds a marker, not even their own.) After hopping out, she turns around and tosses her marker into square 2, where it will stay until her next turn.

The next player must throw his marker into 1, then start by jumping all the way into 3, since he cannot land on a square that hold markers.

Players continue to take turns. Anytime a player throws her marker and misses the right square, lands on the line, jumps in a square where there's a marker--that player's turn is over and the player does not get to advance. The first player to get a marker to segment 8 wins.

In the same way, those who take part in a sport don't receive the winner's crown unless they play by the rules. 2 Timothy 2:5

Thank You God for the fun that we have while we play games. Thank You too that we learn about rules and fairness as we learn to think and have fun. Amen.

Number Rhymes and Finger Plays

Little ones love to wiggle and they love the rhythm of rhymes. Here you have the opportunity to wiggle your fingers and enjoy the language and rhythms of the traditional number rhymes and finger plays listed below.

One, Two, Buckle My Shoe
One, two, buckle my shoe,
Three, four, knock at the door,
Five, six, pick up sticks,
Seven, eight, lay them straight,
Nine, ten, a big fat hen!

One, Two, Three, Four, Five
One, two, three, four, five,
Once I caught a fish alive.
Six, seven, eight, nine, ten,
Then I let him go again.
Why did you let him go?
Because he bit my finger so.
Which finger did he bite?
This little finger on the right.

One, Two, Three, Four
One, two, three, four,
Mary at the cottage door;
Five, six, seven, eight,
Eating cherries off a plate.

The Beehive
Here is the beehive, (Hold up one loosely closed fist.)
Where are the bees? (Hold other hand up questioningly while shrugging your shoulders.)
Hidden away where nobody sees. (Look inside the fist as if it were a telescope.)
Soon they come creeping out of the hive,
One, two, three, four, five! (Open out one finger at a time while counting until all five fingers are open. You can finish by wiggling your fingers, yelling "Tickle bees!" and tickling your little one.)

Two Fat Sausages (finger play)
Two fat sausages (Hold up each thumb "facing" each other.)
Sizzling in the pan. (Wiggle your thumbs.)
One went POP! (Place your index finger in your mouth and pull on your cheek to pop.)
The other went BAM! (Clap your hands together.)

Two Fat Gentlemen

Two fat pigs met in a lane, (Hold up each thumb "facing" each other.)
Bowed most politely, bowed once again. (Bend the thumbs twice.)
How do you do? (Bend the thumbs again.)
How do you do? (Bend the thumbs again.)
And how do you do again? (Bend the thumbs one more time.)
Two thin gentlemen met in a lane, (Two index fingers face each other.)
Bowed most politely and bowed once again. (Bend index fingers twice.)
How do you do? (Bend index fingers.)
How do you do? (Bend index fingers.)
And how do you do again?
Two tall policemen met in a lane, (Middle fingers face each other.)
Bowed most politely, bowed once again. (Continue as before.)
How do you do?
How do you do?
And how do you do again?
Two little school girls met in a lane, ("Ring" fingers face each other.)
Bowed most politely, bowed once again. (Continue as before.)
How do you do?
How do you do?
And how do you do again?
Two little babies met in a lane, (Little fingers face each other.)
Bowed most politely, bowed once again, (Continue as before.)
How do you do?
How do you do?
And how do you do again?

I Saw Three Ships Come Sailing By

I saw three ships come sailing by,
Sailing by,
Sailing by,
I saw three ships come sailing by,
On Christmas Day in the morning.
And what do you think was in them then,
Was in them then,
Was in them then?
And what do you think was in them then,
On Christmas Day in the morning?
Three handsome boys were in them then,
Were in them then,
Were in them then,
Three handsome boys were in them then,
On Christmas Day in the morning.
One could whistle and one could sing
And one could play
on the violin.
Such joy there was at my wedding,
On Christmas Day in the morning.

Four Scarlet Berries

Four scarlet berries
Left upon the tree.
"Thanks," said the blackbird,
"These will do for me."
He ate numbers one and two,
Then ate number three;
When he'd eaten number four,
There was none to see.

Five Little Pussy Cats

Five little pussy cats playing near the door;
One ran and hid inside
And then there were four.
Four little pussy cats underneath a tree;
One heard a dog bark
And then there were three.
Three little pussy cats thinking what to do;
One saw a little bird
And then there were two.
Two little pussy cats sitting in the sun;
One ran to catch his tail
And then there was one.
One little pussy cat looking for some fun;
He saw a butterfly--
And then there was none.

Five Little Peas

Five little peas in a pea-pod pressed, (Hold out one fist.)
One grew, two grew and so did the rest. (Hold up one finger, then two fingers.)
They grew and grew and did not stop, (Hold out your whole hand.)
Until one day the pod went pop! (Hold your hands above your head and clap.)

Six Little Ducks

Six little ducks (Hold up six fingers.)
That I once knew.
Fat ducks, skinny ducks, (Wiggle your six fingers.)
Fair ducks, too.
But the one little duck with a feather on his back, (Hold up one finger.)
He led the others with a quack, quack, quack. (The hand with one finger up is followed with your second hand with all fingers up.)
Down to the river (Place both hands together and move them back and forth.)
They would go
wibble-wobble, wibble wobble,
To and fro.
But the one little duck with a feather on his back, (Hold up one finger.)
He led the others with a quack, quack, quack! (The hand with one finger up is followed with the hand with five fingers up.)
Quack, quack, quack.
Quack, quack, quack.
He led the others with a quack, quack, quack!

Seven Fat Fisherman

Seven fat fishermen,
Sitting side-by-side
Fished from a bridge,
By the banks of the Clyde.
The first caught a tiddler,
The second caught a crab,
The third caught a winkle,
The fourth caught a dab.
The fifth caught a tadpole,
The sixth caught an eel,
But the seventh, he caught
An old spinning wheel.

Eight Seagulls

Eight seagulls flew the midnight sky.
One wailed low and one wailed high.
Another one croaked, another one sighed
Throughout the eerie midnight ride.
One seagull's voice was cackly toned,
Another shrieked, another moaned.
The eighth, much younger than the rest,
Made a happy sound the best.

Engine Number 9

Engine, engine, number nine,
Sliding down Chicago line.
When she's polished, she will shine,
Engine, engine, number nine.

Ten Galloping Horses

Ten galloping horses came through town;
Five were white and five were brown.
They galloped up and galloped down;
Ten galloping horses came through town.

Ten Little Firefighters

Ten little fire fighters sleeping in a row. (Make fists and hold them with the fingers pointing up.)
Ding, ding goes the bell, (Put one fist up in the air and pull down like you are ringing a bell.)
And down the pole they go. (Put both fists in the air, one on top of the other.)
Off on the engine, oh, oh, oh. (Bend arms and move up and down like you are riding in the engine.)
Using the big hose, so, so, so. (Hold both hands out and move back and forth like you are holding a hose.)
When all the fire's out, home so slow. (Hold hands up and grip an imaginary wheel.)
Back into bed, all in a row. (Make fists and hold them with the fingers pointing up.)

 Clap your hands, all you nations. Shout to God with cries of joy. Psalm 47:1

Thank You God for my hands that clap and fingers that wiggle. Thank You for words that rhyme and make us joyful inside. Amen.

Jump Rope Rhymes and Bouncing Ball Games You Can Count On

Even though many children this age cannot yet jump rope, they delight in the nonsense words, rhythm, and counting exercises they provide. Let the children hop in place while saying the rhyme. Adapt the rhymes for little ones by counting how many times you can bounce a ball back and forth. Or drop a "super ball" and count how many bounces it takes. You can really use these rhymes to count anything, anywhere.

Chickety, chickety, chop.
How many times before I stop?
One, two, three, four, five, six, seven, eight, nine, ten.

Candy, Candy in the dish.
How many pieces do you wish?
One, two, three, four, five...

My mother made a chocolate cake.
How many eggs did it take?
One, two, three, four, five.....

Hello, hello, hello, sir.
Meet me at the grocer.
No, sir. Why, sir?
Because I have a cold, sir.
Where did you get the cold, sir?
At the North Pole, sir.
What were you doing there, sir?
Counting polar bears, sir.
How many did you count, sir?
One, two, three, four, five.....

God, your thoughts about me are priceless. No one can possibly add them all up. If I could count them, they would be more than the grains of sand. If I were to fall asleep counting and then wake up, you would still be there with me. Psalm 139:17,18.

Dear God, I can count so many things in this world around me, but I could never count how many times You think about me! Amen.

Devotions You Can Count On

One   Out of all the millions and billions and trillions of stars, raindrops, plants, animals, and people God has created, He has never, ever, ever created anyone just like you. And you know what, there will never, ever, ever be anyone else just like you ever again. Not only did God make you so special that there is just one you in all the world, He knows all about you. The Bible tells us He's had a special plan for you since before you were born. He knows how many hairs are on your head. He knows when you sit down or stand up. He knows when you go somewhere and when you come home. He knows the words you say--even before you say them! We could never count how many thoughts God has about you because we don't have enough numbers to count that high! God has made only one you in all His great universe and He knows everything there is to know about you and loves you more than you could ever imagine.

How you made me is amazing and wonderful. I praise you for that. What you have done is wonderful. I know that very well. Psalm 139:14

Two   When God made the first people, He made two of them: a man and a woman. When Noah took the animals into the ark, the Bible tells us he took them "two by two." He took a boy animal and a girl animal of every kind. All the people and all the animals in the world are either "male", which means a boy or a man, or "female", which means a girl or a woman. So, whether you're a boy or a girl, God said we each are made in His likeness. Inside every boy and girl He creates, God places something very special that comes only from Him and helps us to know His love for us.

So God created human beings in his own likeness. He created them in the likeness of God. He created them as male and female. Genesis 1:27.

Three   The Bible tells us that in all the whole world there are three things that are the most important things we can have. They are faith, hope and love.

Faith is believing what we are told. You have faith when you believe what God says in the Bible. It is believing that God made our whole world and everything in it. It's believing that He loves us and sent Jesus to show us what God is like. It is believing that Jesus is God's Son and trusting Him to forgive us for the bad things we have done that make God sad so that we will be God's children too and live with Him forever in heaven one day.

Hope is believing good things will happen. God has promised that we will live forever with Him if we believe in Jesus and obey him. That's not just a good thing--it's the best thing in the world!

Love is treating each other with kindness. It is waiting for someone without complaining. It is wanting good things for the one you love. The Bible tells us that out of these three most important things, love is the best.

The three most important things to have are faith, hope and love. But the greatest of them is love. 1 Corinthians 13:13

Four   Many, many years ago there was a king who didn't know God and didn't worship him. He made a giant golden statue and ordered all the people to bow down and worship the statue as a god. Shadrach, Meshach, and Abednego wouldn't worship the statue because they knew we are only to worship God. This made the king very angry and he ordered them to be thrown into a very large, very hot fire. He watched to see if they would burn but instead of seeing three men in the fire, he saw four, and the fourth looked like an angel of God! The king called for the men to come out. He praised God who had kept Shadrach, Meshach, and Abednego safe with his special angel in the fire.

Didn't we throw three men into the fire?...Look! I see four men walking around in the fire. They aren't tied up. And the fire hasn't even harmed them. Daniel 3:24b, 25

Five   A long time ago a mommy packed her son a picnic lunch to eat when he went to listen to Jesus teach. She put five pieces of bread in that lunch and two small fish. It was just the right size for a growing boy. Not everybody who came to listen to Jesus planned ahead the way that boy's mommy did. Over 5,000 people, as many people as live in some towns, came and listened all day without having anything to eat! Jesus and His friends didn't want the people to go home hungry and the boy offered the lunch his mommy packed to help. Jesus blessed his lunch and those five pieces of bread and two fish fed 5,000 people. They even had food left over! Jesus still blesses us when we share what we have with Him and those around us.

Here is a boy with five small loaves of barley bread. He also has two small fish. But how far will that go in such a large crowd?....Then Jesus took the loaves and gave thanks. He handed out the bread to those who were seated. He gave them as much as they wanted. And he did the same with the fish. John 6:8b-1

Six   A miracle is an amazing wonderful thing that only God can do. Jesus did many miracles while He lived on this earth. He made sick people well with just the touch of His hand, He fed 5,000 people with just a few pieces of food, and He changed six big jars full of water into six big jars full of wine for a special feast. Jesus didn't do these miracles just to show off. Jesus did miracles to show the people that He really is the Son of God and to show them how much God cares about us.

Six stone water jars stood nearby...Jesus said to the servants, "Fill the jars with water...Take it to the person in charge of the dinner." They did what he said. The person in charge tasted the water that had been turned into wine...That was the first of Jesus' miraculous signs. John 2:6a,7a,8b,9,11

Seven   God created this whole big beautiful world. The Bible says He created everything we see in seven days.

On day one He made light and called it "day" and darkness and called it "night." On day two He made the sky. On day three He made the land and oceans and plants to grow on the land. On day four He made the sun and the moon. On day five He filled the waters with fish and sea creatures and He filled the sky with birds. On day six He made all the land animals and then He made people. When He was finished making our world, He said it was very good. On the seventh day, He rested.

So the heavens and the earth and everything in them were completed. By the seventh day God had finished the work he had been doing. So on the seventh day he rested from all of his work. Genesis 2:1-2

Eight   Did you know there was once a king who began ruling when he was only eight years old? His name was Josiah and the Bible said he did what was right. When he grew up, he made sure that God's temple was repaired from the damage that had been done when bad kings had ruled the land. While they were fixing the temple, the priests found a scroll in the temple with the laws God wanted them to follow written on it. Josiah obeyed God and made sure the people of Israel obeyed Him too. Josiah was a good king and God tells us about him in the Bible as an example of someone who pleased Him--even when he was a child.

Josiah was eight years old when he became king...He did what was right in the eyes of the Lord. 2 Chronicles 34:1a, 2a.

Nine   Do your parents remind you to say "Please" and "Thank you"? Sometimes it doesn't seem like a very important thing to do but the Bible tells us that after nine men forgot to say "Thank you" to Jesus, He was sad.

Jesus had made ten men well. They all had a terrible sickness and had been forced to leave their families and live in caves away from all the cities and towns. Once Jesus made them well, nine of them ran back to their homes and never came back to say thank you. One person didn't forget. Before he ran home to his family, before he did anything else, this man told Jesus "Thank you."

We should also remember to thank Jesus for all the good things He does for us.

When one of them saw that he was healed, he came back. He praised God in a loud voice. He threw himself at Jesus' feet and thanked him...Jesus asked,"...Where are the other nine?" Luke 17:15,16,17b

Ten   Jesus told many stories to help people understand how important each one of us is to God. One of His stories was about a woman who had ten silver coins. She lost one of those ten coins and she searched and searched and searched for it. Jesus said she lit bright lamps and swept her entire house until she found the lost coin. After she found that coin, the lady called all her friends and neighbors together and had a party to celebrate finding the lost coin.

Jesus said that God looks for each one of us to tell us that He loves us. When we choose to live our lives for God, He celebrates just like the lady who found the one coin she had lost.

Or suppose a woman has ten silver coins and loses one. She will light a lamp and sweep the house. She will search carefully until she finds the coin. And when she finds it, she will call her friends and neighbors together. She will say, "Be joyful with me."...I tell you, it is the same in heaven. Luke 15:8, 9a, 10.

Eleven   Sometimes people say and do things to us that hurt us. Sometimes they hurt us with things and sometimes they hurt us with words. The Bible tells us that a boy named Joseph had eleven brothers. Joseph's brothers didn't like him very much and did some very mean things to Joseph that hurt him. They sold him to people who took him to another country and made him work as a slave. But Joseph obeyed God and lived the way God wanted him to and God blessed Joseph. Joseph became a great ruler in the country where he lived. He even helped save his family when they didn't have enough food to eat. God promised Joseph, and He promises us, that God can take things that hurt us and one day make something good come of them.

But Joseph said to them," Don't be afraid...You planned to harm me. But God planned it for good. Genesis 50:19-20

We know that in all things God works for the good of those who love him.   Roman 8:28a

Twelve   Jesus chose twelve special friends to be with Him as he traveled and taught people about God. These special friends were called His disciples. They followed Him wherever He went. They listened to the things He taught. They remembered what He said and, later, told other people about Jesus and His teaching. They tried to obey Jesus and do the things He asked of them.

We can be Jesus' disciples today. When we study the Bible and try to do the things God wants us to do, we are Jesus' disciples. When we love Jesus and tell others about Him, we are His disciples too.

When morning came, he called for his disciples to come to him. He chose 12 of them. Luke 6:13a.

You must go and make disciples of all nations. Matthew 28:19a.

39

ACTIVITY PAGES FOR NUMBERS 1-12

 1 ONE 1 ONE 1 ONE 1 ONE 1 ONE 1 ONE 1 ONE 1 ONE 1 ONE 1

Directions: draw your face in the circle below. Draw your eyes, your nose, your mouth, your hair, your ears...anything you want to show the special person God made when He made you!

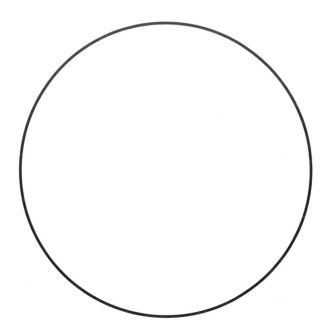

Practice writing the number 1.

Draw a circle.

Directions: circle the one mirror you like the best. Draw your face inside it.

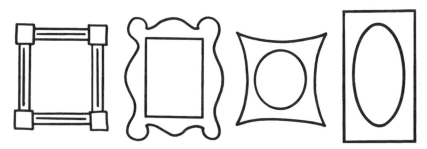

Directions: Draw a line from each animal to its mate.

Practice writing the number 2.

Draw 2 snakes.

Directions: Color or decorate three hearts

Practice writing the number 3.

Draw three triangles.

Directions: Cut out the squares along the black lines. Glue or tape them onto the men in the correct order. (Note to Teacher: See Devotion for Number Four on page 37.)

Practice writing the number 4.

Draw four squares.

Directions: These fish need stripes. Draw the number of stripes on each fish that matches the number on the paper next to it.

Practice writing the number 5.

5 5 5

Directions: Find all the fish that have stars. Place an x on each of the fish that has a star.

Write how many fish that have stars here:

_____

Directions: Draw a line from the water pot to the stem with the matching number of grapes on it.

Practice writing the number 6.

Directions: Write the number of jewels each goblet has on the line to the right.

7 SEVEN 7 SEVEN 7 SEVEN 7 SEVEN 7 SEVEN 7 SEVEN 7 SEVEN 7

Directions: Count the items in each row and write the number that tells how many are in the row at the end of the line.

Practice writing the number 7.

46

Directions: Fill in the missing numbers on the scroll.

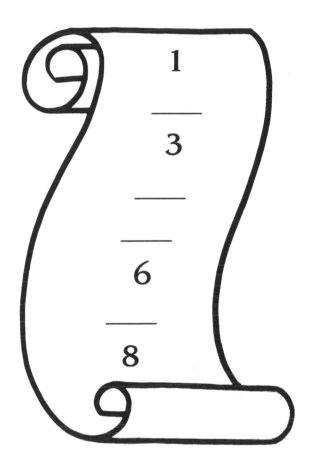

1

___

3

___

___

6

___

8

Practicing writing the number 8.

Directions: Draw eight jewels on King Josiah's crown.

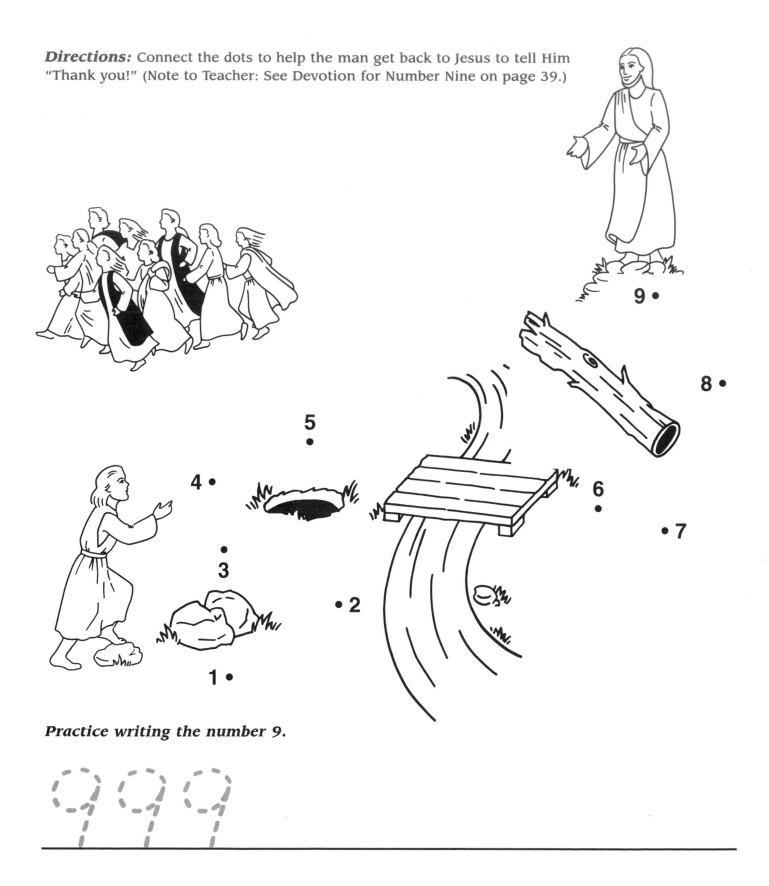

Directions: Connect the dots to help the man get back to Jesus to tell Him "Thank you!" (Note to Teacher: See Devotion for Number Nine on page 39.)

9•

8•

5
•

4•

6
•

•7

3
•

•2

1•

Practice writing the number 9.

Directions: Oh no! The woman has spilled all ten coins this time. Can you help her find the coins? Circle or draw an X on each coin ⊙ you find. Did you find all ten? (Note to Teacher: See Devotion for Number Ten on page 39.)

Practice writing the number 10.

Directions: Circle 10 coins.

Directions: Write in the missing numbers on Joseph's brothers. (Note to Teacher: See Devotion for Number Eleven on page 39.)

Practice writing the number 11.

Directions: Which box of lollipops should Sarah buy if she wants to give each of her 12 friends a lollipop? Draw a circle around that box.

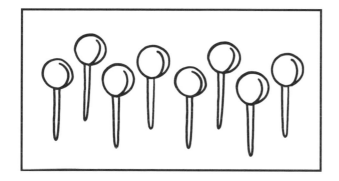

Practice writing the number 12.